Everybody Feels...

Happy

Jane Bingham

Crabtree Publishing Company

www.crabtreebooks.com

Published by Crabtree Publishing Company

Copyright © 2008

www.crabtreebooks.com

PMB16A
350 Fifth Ave., Suite 3308
New York, NY 10118

616 Welland Ave.
St. Catharines, Ontario
L2M 5V6

First published in hardcover in the U.S.A. in 2006 by QEB Publishing, Inc.

Cataloging-in-Publication data is available at the Library of Congress.

ISBN 10: 0-7787-4065-X paperback
ISBN 13: 978-0-7787-4065-0 paperback

Written by Jane Bingham
Illustrations Helen Turner
Designed by Alix Wood
Editor Clare Weaver

Publisher Steve Evans
Editorial Director Jean Coppendale
Art Director Zeta Davies

Printed and bound in China

Contents

Feeling happy

People have lots of different **feelings**.

Sometimes they feel sad.

LOST

Sparky

But often, they feel happy.

How do you think
Ellie feels now?

Everybody likes feeling happy.
What kinds of things make you happy?

How does it feel?

When you are happy, you feel warm inside—even if it's raining!

Sometimes being happy
makes you feel **excited**.

7

Sometimes it makes you feel **peaceful** and **calm**.

When you are happy, everything feels great.

What makes you happy?

All kinds of things make people feel happy.

Here's what happened to Holly and Joe.

Holly's story

My name is Holly and
I love parties.

The week before my birthday,
I made **invitations** for all my friends.

I asked them to come to a **costume** party.

Making invitations was really fun.

Then I helped Mom make my costume.

It was really **tricky**,
but it made us
laugh a lot.

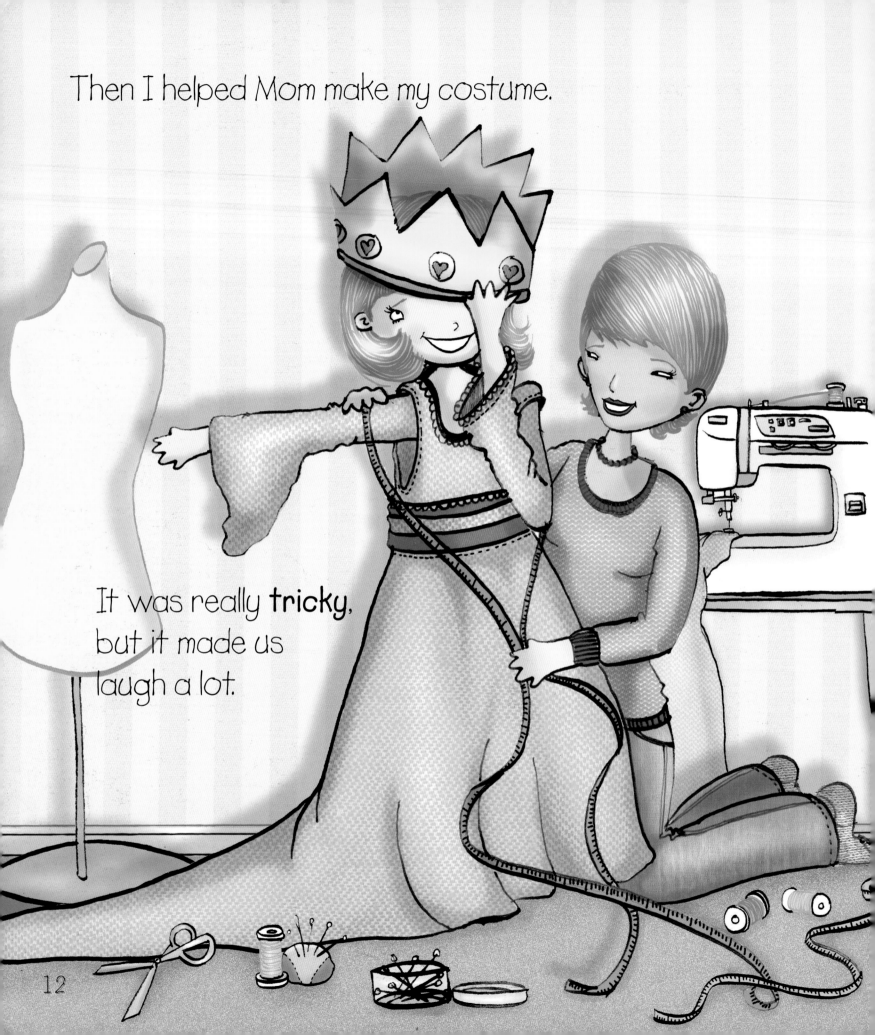

The day before the party,
I helped **decorate** the cake.

It looked great!

At my party, we played lots of games.
Then we had a **delicious** lunch.

I was so happy,

I couldn't stop smiling!

Joe's story

I'm Joe. One morning, Mom woke us up very early.

We all got into the car. It was very exciting.

Dad didn't tell us where we were going.

We drove for miles,
and miles, and
miles...

until we saw the ocean!

Then we all rushed down to the beach.

I jumped over

some **huge** waves.

It felt great!

We looked in some rock pools and saw a tiny crab.

Then we had a picnic.

In the afternoon, we built a pirate ship out of sand.

It was the best day I've ever had!

Sharing happiness

Happiness can be **infectious**.

When you smile at people, it makes them feel **cheerful**.

Helping other people makes them happy...

and it makes you feel happy, too.

Glossary

calm if you're calm, you feel peaceful and you're not worried about anything

cheerful if you're cheerful, you feel happy and you often have a smile on your face

costume a costume is a set of clothes that you wear to make yourself look different

decorate when you decorate something, you add things to it to make it look nice

delicious food that is delicious tastes very good

excited if you're excited, you feel very lively and happy

feelings your feelings tell you how you are and what kind of mood you're in

huge something that is huge is very big

infectious if something is infectious, it can be passed easily from person to person

invitation when you send someone an invitation, you ask them to do something with you

peaceful if you're peaceful, you feel calm and you don't want to race around

tricky if something is tricky, it's hard to do

Index

Notes for parents and teachers

- Look at the front cover of the book together. Talk about the picture. Can your children guess what the book is going to be about? Read the title together.

- Read the first line on page 4: "People have lots of different feelings." Help your children to make a list of different feelings.

- Ask your children to draw some simple faces showing different feelings. Then talk about them. Which feelings make you feel good? Which don't feel so good?

- Read about what happened to Ellie (pages 4–5). Talk about Ellie's feelings—first, when she lost Sparky, and then when she found him.

- Talk to your children about feeling happy and sad. Is it possible for people to feel happy all the time?

- Read the question on page 5: "What kind of things make you happy?" Help your children to make a list of things that make them happy.

- Read about feeling happy on page 6. Then ask your children to draw a picture of how they feel when they're happy.

- Look at page 7. Think about the feelings of everyone in the picture. How do Ellie and her brother feel? How do their grandma and grandpa feel?

- Talk about feeling excited and happy—like Ellie and her brother on page 7. Can your children remember times when they have felt like this? (Possibly at Christmas, or when they had a friend stay over.)

- Look at page 8. Can your children remember some peaceful, happy times?

- Ask your children what they like about parties. Then read Holly's story (pages 10–14). Talk about getting ready for a party.

- Read Joe's story together (pages 15–19). Then talk to your children about going on vacation. What do they like about vacations?

- Think about the nice surprise that Joe's dad gave him. Help your children to plan a nice surprise for somebody they know.

- Read pages 20–21 together. Talk with your children about how it feels when you make someone happy.

- Help your children to think of ways to make the people around them feel happy.